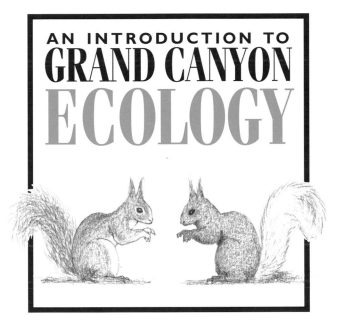

AN INTRODUCTION TO
GRAND CANYON
ECOLOGY

by
Rose Houk

with illustrations by
Tony Brown

Grand Canyon Association
Grand Canyon, Arizona

ISBN 0-938216-54-6
Library of Congress Card Catalog Number 96-078108
First Edition

Cover photography—Muav Canyon, Grand Canyon North Rim,
by George H.H. Huey

Book designed by Christina Watkins
Typography and production by Amanda Summers
Lithography by Lorraine Press, Inc.

✪ Printed on recycled paper using vegatable-based inks.

*Proceeds from the sale of this book directly benefit Grand
Canyon National Park.*

Acknowledgments
Many people played a part in giving life to this book. First and
foremost is Christina Watkins, who conceptualized it and whose
vision guided it from inception to completion. Pam Frazier at
Grand Canyon Association patiently guided it every step along
the winding path to publication. Sandra Scott applied sharp
editorial skills. Tony Brown contributed enthusiasm and
insights; his illustrations, which grace the book's pages, portray
more than words ever could. Amanda Summers provided
patience and creativity. Much gratitude goes to biologists and
ecologists who have shared their knowledge and ideas, directly
or indirectly, knowingly and unknowingly: Sylvester Allred,
Robert Balling, Bryan Brown, Nancy Brian, Steve Carothers,
Jim Mead, Margaret Moore, Mike Rabe, Larry Stevens, Bob
Webb, Tom Whitham, and the dedicated HawkWatchers. Help
also came from several members of the staff of Grand Canyon
National Park, including Carl Bowman, Jesse Duhnkrack,
Elaine Leslie, and Daniel Spotsky, as well as Anita Davis and
Greer Price, who undertook careful reviews of the manuscript.
And finally to Michael, who has shared a love of the Grand
Canyon for so many years.

R.H.

CONTENTS

In the end, we will conserve only what we love, we will love only what we understand, and we will understand only what we are taught.

—Baba Dioum, Senegalese conservationist

CANYON HOME

The Grand Canyon is an ecosystem... dynamic, open, and ongoing.

On a fine day in late September, I perch on a limestone ledge at Lipan Point on the South Rim of Grand Canyon. It's a place I frequent for its stunning views. Across the canyon, sculpted from the rock walls of the North Rim, pose flat-topped Wotans Throne and the sharpened pinnacle of Vishnu Temple.

A mile below, the Colorado River arcs elegantly around the delta of Unkar Creek, flowing in from the north side. The waves of Hance Rapid, the first really big whitewater on the river, are visible downstream. The rapid's congestion of boulders and roil of waves mark a tumultuous entry into the narrow, dark depths of the canyon's Inner Gorge.

Suddenly, I glimpse movement off my left shoulder. It's a sharp-shinned hawk, soaring in an alcove, a small dot counterposed against the immensity of the canyon. With binoculars, I follow the gray silhouette of the bird as it circles skyward, catches a thermal, and makes a beeline over the tops of the pinyon trees, bound for the San Francisco Peaks etched on the southern horizon. The hawk, perhaps headed for the tropics of Central America, is following some ancient sense ordering its departure from the north country for the winter.

Lipan Point on the South Rim.

The presence of the hawk flying over Lipan Point reminded me that Grand Canyon is more than a geologic paradise. Seen from the rims, the canyon can appear two dimensional, a static world of timeless, unmoving rock. First-time visitors stand in disbelieving awe, overwhelmed by the canyon's sheer size, its infinity of buttes, mesas, ridges, cliffs, slopes, amphitheaters, and side canyons, its epic silence. To help comprehend the place, a visitor attends a geology talk, then goes back out and stares at the canyon, trying to repeat the names of all those rocks in neat horizontal layers, trying to imagine that the seemingly tiny stream a mile below carved this defile.

e•col•o•gy (e-kol´e-je) The science of the relationships between organisms and their environments. Also called "bionomics."

What may not be apparent on that first visit is that Grand Canyon is alive with plants and animals engaged in a tightly choreographed dance: birds, bats, snakes, scorpions, cactus, lizards, frogs, toads, fish, deer, mountain lions, squirrels, lichens, fungi, and an uncounted host of others.

The metallic whir of broad-tailed hummingbirds is a familiar sound in North Rim meadows in summer. These tiny, frenetic birds arrive as the gilia and penstemons start to bloom. Bird and flower fit hand-in-glove, providing an excellent example of a coevolutionary relationship in which both have adapted in concert over millions of years to suit each other's needs.

Canyon Statistics

Size: 1.2 million acres

River length: 277 miles

Plants: 1,500 species

Fish: 26 species

Amphibians: 6 species

Reptiles: 35 species

Mammals: 76 species

Birds: 305 species

Insects: unknown

Grand Canyon is an *ecosystem*, a collection of plants and animals coexisting in time and space, interacting with one another and with their environment. Like all ecosystems, it is dynamic, open, and ongoing, making for infinite complexity. As an ecosystem, the canyon is especially complex because it is so big—a million acres of land and 277 miles of river—and because it contains so many different environments and organisms: at latest count 1,500 species of plants, 26 species of fish, 6 species of amphibians, 35 species of reptiles, 76 species of mammals, 305 species of birds, and an unknown number of insect species. Even the most sophisticated computer models cannot describe or measure all the species and their potential relationships. We must also take into account that the canyon is not an island but

Lake Mead

SHIVWITS PLATEAU

Tuwee

Colorado River

part of a larger whole—its forests, deserts, and river do not begin and end in the canyon.

The word *ecology* was coined in 1866 by Ernst Haeckel from Greek words meaning "study of the home." Ecology is the study of ecosystems, which are the synthesis of the *abiotic*, or "nonliving" world of rock, soil, moisture, temperature, and sunlight, and the association, or assemblage, of all *biotic* organisms. A big subject for a big place like Grand Canyon.

Through the first part of the twentieth century, the focus of ecology was on hard science, attempting to measure various interactions. Because ecosystems are so dynamic, ecologists found such measurements difficult to perform, and they began to look at smaller pieces of the puzzle. Then, in 1962, biologist and writer Rachel Carson

The Grand Canyon is not an island but part of a larger whole. The forests, deserts, and the Colorado River do not begin and end in the canyon.

KAIBAB PLATEAU

Grand Canyon National Park

Colorado River

● Grand Canyon Lodge

North Rim

ONINO PLATEAU

● South Rim ●

Grand Canyon Village

Desert View

Within an ecological community are food chains, actually complex, intertwined webs. A portion of a web can be isolated and drawn as a pyramid, showing *trophic levels*, essentially who eats whom in an ecosystem; or, more scientifically, how energy flows through the system. The word *trophic* comes from the Greek word for food. At the base of a food web are the green plants, or producers. In nature's economy, green plants are the proletariat supporting the entire structure of any ecosystem. Above the producers are the consumers, or herbivores, which eat plants. It takes many producers to support a lesser number of consumers. At the apex of the pyramid are the final consumers, the carnivores, the fewest in number and often the biggest in size. At all levels are the mostly invisible, but critical, decomposers—fungi, bacteria, mites, and springtails that work largely on and underground to break down organic material. Their services are critical because they cycle nutrients back into the soil upon which green plants can draw.

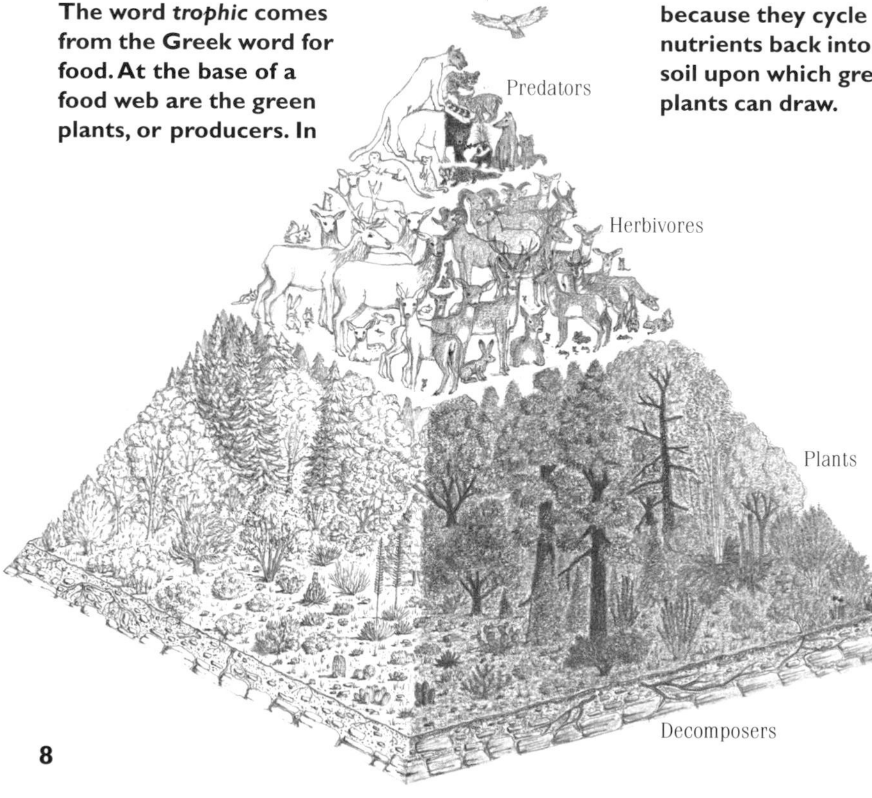

Predators

Herbivores

Plants

Decomposers

published her book *Silent Spring*. In it, she warned of the dangers to wildlife of pesticide use. Publication of the book marked a turning point: ecology became a political movement that catapulted the fates of tiny fish and unknown plants to the forefront of the world's attention. Ecology became a household word.

Rachel Carson in 1965.

How organisms interact— in competition, cooperation, or neutral coexistence—and what adaptations they have evolved to survive are all within the realm of the subject known as ecology. Ecology deals with process—the daily, seasonal, and annual events that mark the lives of living things—birth, growth, migration, death, decay, and renewal. Ecology also concerns itself with the cycling of energy: green plants converting sunlight (and other materials) into food, that in turn feeds animals, that eventually die and decompose to furnish nutrients that replenish the system. Finally, ecology looks at patterns—where plants and animals live and why. How to explain the cactus here, the mule deer there?

Teasing out some of the intriguing stories and relationships, we can begin to gain a glimmer of understanding of this great ecosystem called Grand Canyon.

From an energy standpoint, ecosystems are highly inefficient. At each step along the trophic pyramid, 80 to 90 percent of energy is lost. Overall, only a fraction, about one percent, of the Sun's energy is actually captured and used.

FROM THE BOTTOM UP

Climate has always been the single most profound influence on the ecology of Grand Canyon.

Clarence Dutton was a smitten man. While exploring the North Rim in 1880 and 1881, this poetic geologist pronounced Grand Canyon "the sublimest thing on earth. It is so not alone by virtue of its magnitude, but by virtue of the whole—its ensemble." So stunning was the panorama at one spot that Dutton named it Point Sublime.

The point is worthy of the name, for the 270-degree view there is, to my mind, unequaled in all of Grand Canyon. To reach Point Sublime requires

The panorama from Point Sublime, by artist William Henry Holmes with the Dutton expedition in 1880.

some effort, bumping along many miles of a single-track dirt road. One August day, my husband and I decided to make the journey. From the somber spruce and fir forest we emerged to see stunted pinyon and juniper trees clinging to the rim, joined by sticky cliffrose, silvery sagebrush, and littleleaf mountain mahogany. Waspish tarantula hawks floated from the branches of the pinyons. White-throated swifts and violet-green swallows darted over the void of the canyon. Black ants scurried furtively over the rocky ground.

With the expansive view, we could clearly see a large rain cell tracking across the canyon from south to north, moving up the gaping drainage of Crystal Creek. Lightning snaked from cloud to ground, and I kept close watch on its distance from us. A few big raindrops fell, but the storm never materialized into much. All afternoon we watched storm cells form and reform. At sunset, diaphanous veils of rain glowed in soft peach over the western end of the canyon. Lightning flashed from within the clouds like giant lightbulbs switching on and off. To the east, the slanting rays of light painted the red walls of the canyon an intense crimson.

Summer storm over Grand Canyon.

Such sweeping summer storms exemplify the greatest influence on the Grand Canyon ecosystem: climate. The canyon is viewed as a "bottom up" ecosystem, one in which physical aspects structure the biological world. Precipitation and temperature, and especially the extremes of each, are the biggest determiners of what vegetation grows and, correspondingly, what animals can live here. (In contrast, a "top-down" ecosystem, such as a coral reef, is shaped by a biological entity.)

The long hand of climate reaches down and touches every aspect of the living canyon. Rain and snow feed the Colorado River and sidestreams, whose flows deepen and widen the canyon. Climate shapes the survival strategies of organisms and controls key physical factors such as geology, topography, and soils.

Weathered rock and decomposing plant material go together to make soil, the medium

Lightning is simply a giant spark between oppositely charged particles—in-cloud and cloud-to-ground.

Coarse, loose soils allow larger plants to grow, above; fine, heavier soils support smaller, dense plants like meadow grasses, below.

through which plants absorb moisture and nutrients. The amount of moisture and degree of slope help determine the rate of soil formation. And while overall amounts of rainfall are important, what is even more important is how much of that moisture is available to plants' roots. Coarse, loose sandstone and limestone soils more readily release moisture to plants than do fine, heavy clays or shales—thus larger shrubs and trees grow on terraced bouldery slopes, while grassy meadows are characteristic of heavy, waterlogged valley soils. Minerals in soil are also of significance to plants, determining what can grow where. Saltbush, for instance, can tolerate salty soils, while prince's plume is an indicator of selenium in the soil.

Grand Canyon offers an extreme range of elevation, from 9,200 feet at its highest point on the North Rim to 1,200 feet at the lowest point near Lake Mead. With this radical topographic relief come wide variations in moisture and temperature. Average annual precipitation on the North Rim is 25 inches (with snowfall often averaging 125 inches a year). At the South Rim, a thousand feet lower than the North Rim, precipitation averages 15 inches a year. Down in the canyon at Phantom Ranch, it decreases to 9 inches a year, and dwindles to a scant 6 inches in the far western desert.

Temperatures from the rims into the inner canyon likewise display great differences. The North Rim is the place to be in summer, where daytime highs are usually in the eighties; on the South Rim they rarely exceed ninety degrees Fahrenheit. But as any hiker, mule rider, or river runner knows, the inner canyon is a scorcher in the summer. It gets hotter and hotter as you descend into the canyon, with temperatures commonly topping the one-hundred-degree mark through July and August and into September. Heat waves shimmer off the black schist of the Inner Gorge, and plants and animals pretty much shut down in the daytime.

On the other hand, while winter temperatures on the rims hover around freezing, the inner canyon is often a balmy twenty degrees warmer. This is not to say it doesn't get cold down in the canyon. My first winter working at the canyon, I was determined to spend Christmas at Phantom Ranch. Friends and I carried in a whole frozen chicken to bake in the oven at the ranger dorm. When we arrived, the chicken was still frozen; so we ate a simple canned dinner that night. Surely, the bird would be thawed by the time we hiked back up to Indian Garden, and we could cook it there. But it wasn't, and we had another meager dinner, not exactly a Christmas repast to remember.

Christmas 12,000 years ago in the canyon was strikingly different. Had we been hiking then, we might have seen 300-pound ground sloths nibbling globemallow, giant vultures soaring in search of carrion, furry little marmots whistling from boulders, and shaggy, white-haired mountain goats tripping along the steep slopes. It was the ice age.

At their fullest extent 23,000 to 18,000 years ago, glaciers covered most of Canada and the northern United States. Although glaciers never actually blanketed this part of the Southwest, their presence in the higher mountains and to the north made for an overall colder, wetter climate. Reverberations of the ice age were felt throughout the depths of Grand Canyon.

The canyon contains thousands of dry, dusty caves with deep deposits of animal dung and bones undisturbed since prehistoric times. It also holds other treasures left by a busy little rodent, the packrat. Packrats cache bones, dung, and plant parts in their nests, glue them together with their urine, and thus preserve these fossil remains for scientists, called paleoecologists, to sniff out. From the packrat nests and cave deposits, a fairly detailed picture of past climates of Grand Canyon can be drawn.

In Rampart Cave in the far western end of the canyon near Lake Mead, geologists and paleoecologists have found world-class deposits of softball-sized lumps of dung left by Shasta ground sloths. The sloths flourished in the region until 11,000 years ago, when the last one became extinct. Tragically, in 1976 people started a fire in the cave, destroying nearly all the precious sloth dung. Stantons Cave, two hundred forty miles upstream in Marble Canyon, is another treasure chest, containing bones, hair, and horns from an amazing menagerie of prehistoric fauna—a huge vulture called Merriam's teratorn, an extinct turkey, a condor, a sage grouse, a clay-colored robin known today in the tropics of Mexico, a vampire bat, and the Harrington's mountain goat, which became extinct about the same time as the Shasta ground sloth. Plant material entombed in Stantons Cave shows that a woodland of juniper, sagebrush, and shadscale once grew in the eastern end of

Before the full glacial, the inner canyon was an open woodland. During the full glacial, junipers, along with desert shrubs, reached the banks of the Colorado River. Between 18,000 and 10,000 years ago, the open woodland again assumed dominance. Animals of the inner canyon were an interesting mix of large grazing mammals, now extinct, to snakes and lizards we still find today.

the canyon. Around the cave now are typical modern desert plants: agave, Mormon tea, and cactus.

Why did the ground sloth, mountain goat, and other big animals become extinct? What happened around 11,000 years ago to bring about their demise? Two different views are under lively debate. One involves the possibility that prehistoric hunters swept in from the north and killed off the megafauna. The other looks to the shift from juniper and ash to agave and cactus and sees climate change as the cause.

During the ice age, winter was the rainy season in Grand Canyon. And both winters and summers were cooler. As the glaciers receded between 12,000 and 9,000 years ago, climate became hotter and drier, and precipitation began to shift to today's two-season pattern. The ranges of individual plant species moved upward and northward. Finally, by 8,000 years ago, a distinct warming trend had become established all over the Southwest, inspiring the evolution of all the major deserts of North America.

Packrat middens are museums of past flora and fauna.

Climate has always been the single most profound influence on the ecology of Grand Canyon. When we realize that climate has changed, and that humans were affecting the ecosystem even that far back in time, we realize what we see today is only a snapshot in time. With that realization, the story of Grand Canyon ecology becomes even more dynamic and complex—and more interesting.

Summer

Winter

Predominant directions of seasonal storm movement toward Grand Canyon National Park.

The central feature of Grand Canyon climate is the two-season pattern of precipitation—moisture comes both in summer and in winter in a nearly even fifty-fifty split. Summer monsoons are generated in the Gulf of California and the Gulf of Mexico when high pressure forms in the upper atmosphere. As the center of that high pressure shifts north-ward, the air is lifted over the Mogollon Rim south of the canyon, cools, condenses, and settles around northern Arizona. The time is ripe for the monsoons to begin, traditionally sometime in July. On summer mornings, as temperatures rise and the land heats up, anvil-topped cumulus clouds tower 40,000 feet into the sky. Conditions change suddenly on these days. By noon, lightning and thunder-storms shake the

heavens and the earth. It's the time of year when you want to avoid hiking or camping *in* a sidestream in the canyon, for flashfloods are common.

Winter storms, not surprisingly, come from the north and the west. They normally originate in the northern Pacific. As the storms migrate eastward, they bring rain in the canyon and snow to the rims. While summer rains come in local bursts, winter precipitation is steadier and more widespread. These big, regional systems sit for several days, coloring the sky a cold pewter and sometimes creating cloud inversions in the canyon.

WEBS

The Grand Canyon is alive with plants and animals engaged in a tightly choreographed dance.

C. Hart Merriam, biologist.

In 1889 C. Hart Merriam took a hike into Grand Canyon. He spent two nights there in mid September, losing sleep because marauding cactus mice tugged at his blanket and tried to steal his food. Head of the United States Biological Survey, Merriam had come to northern Arizona to investigate the region's plants and animals. For a couple of months, he and fellow biologists camped on the San Francisco Peaks near Flagstaff, climbed to their summit, poked into the Painted Desert, and visited the inner canyon.

The diversity was what interested Merriam. In only eighty miles' distance, from the highest point on the peaks to the bottom of the canyon, Merriam experienced 10,000 feet of elevation loss. Compressed in that distance, he saw the biological equivalent of a journey from the Arctic to Mexico.

Though brief, Merriam's trip was significant. During his stay, he observed and mapped major "life zones"—alpine tundra at the top of the peaks, Canadian and Hudsonian spruce-fir forests, the Transition Zone of ponderosa pine, the Upper Sonoran Zone of pinyon and juniper woodland, and the Lower Sonoran Zone of desert shrubs and trees in the bottom of Grand Canyon.

Though now considered a little old-fashioned and too simplistic, the life-zone concept was revolutionary for its time. While Merriam's contemporaries were describing and naming individual plants and animals, he was formulating an idea that looked at *communities* of plants and animals. He also suggested that an environmental influence—

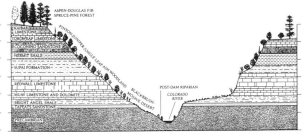

temperature— governed the inhabitants found in a community. Merriam later realized that temperature alone could not explain everything.

Succeeding generations of ecologists have expanded and modified Merriam's ideas. Distinct altitudinal boundaries between communities are not as clearcut as Merriam first drew them. Ecologists are fond of charting *gradients*— changes in things such as light, elevation, temperature, and precipitation—and how they relate to plants and animals. Sometimes gradients are sharp, sometimes gradual. Fine-scale mapping of the canyon's vegetation in recent years has shown more than sixty associations of plants in the park. Colored on a map, these associations look more like a lovely tile mosaic than sharply striped zones.

C. Hart Merriam's original life-zone concept, based largely on temperature, has been modified over the years. Plant communities, mapped in eastern and central Grand Canyon (below) form a mosaic reflecting not only temperature, but light, elevation, moisture, and slope exposure as well.

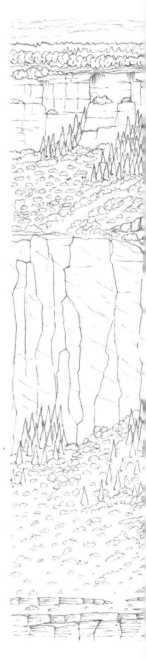

One condition that enhances the plant mosaic is *slope aspect,* the direction a slope faces. South-facing slopes receive more sunlight and have less soil moisture, thus they are hotter and drier than north-facing slopes. A general example is the occurrence of timberline in mountains, above which trees will not grow. Timberline is usually several hundred feet lower on the colder north side of a mountain than on the warmer south side. Slope aspect produces local differences that can alter any altitudinal "rules" applied to plant zones. Because of it, desert shrubs can be found growing near forest trees.

On the South Rim of Grand Canyon, visitors can see tall green conifers rising in sheltered cliffsides just below the rim. These are Douglas-firs, trees normally found at higher elevations. The cool, moist conditions of north-facing alcoves create a microclimate allowing Douglas-firs to become established.

Douglas-fir is neither a true fir nor a hemlock, though its genus name, *Pseudotsuga,* translates as "false hemlock." Mouse-tail tips on the cones distinguish it from the true firs.

Life on the brink
Warm air rising up
out of the canyon
creates a microclimate
on the edges of the
rims and sustains
plants normally found
at lower elevations.

Given that nature draws few hard lines, we can still look at broad communities. Ecologists do this all the time, especially with communities of characteristic plants and animals. In the Grand Canyon ecosystem, we find several *biotic communities:* the boreal forest and mountain meadows of the North Rim; the ponderosa forest on the North and South rims; pinyon-juniper woodland and mountain scrub-chaparral on the slopes below the rims; desert scrub of the inner canyon; and riparian areas where water is present—springs and seeps, marshes, sidestreams, and the Colorado River.

Boreal Forests & Mountain Meadows

At the highest elevations of the North Rim, above 8,700 feet, is the boreal zone, named for Boreas, god of the north wind, whose breath is felt most distinctly here. The tall evergreens that grow here are a southern extension of the classic forests of the Rocky Mountains. In this storybook forest, the dominant tree species are Engelmann spruce, alpine and white firs, Douglas-fir, and ponderosa pine. Lovely quaking aspens are interspersed throughout, in autumn casting their golden light among the deep blue-green of the forest. Snow usually covers the ground six or seven months of the year.

Coolness and moisture shape this forest, and the dense, shaded conditions prevent the growth of many flowers or shrubs beneath the trees. The needles and other material that fall to the ground decay slowly in the cold; what soil is

The conifer forest of the North Rim is a southern extension of the classic forests of the Rocky Mountains.

formed tends to be acidic due to the chemistry of conifer needles.

The boreal forest possesses a distinct coterie of birds, each species selecting a different layer of forest in which to forage for seeds and insects. Blue grouse inhabit the forest floor, nibbling needles, seeds, buds, and twigs shed by the spruce and fir. The northern three-toed woodpecker, a rare bird, prefers dead snags and tree trunks. In summer, ruby-crowned kinglets and boisterous Clark's nutcrackers frequent the tops of the trees.

Interrupting the solid wall of forest on the North Rim are open, grassy meadows. Again, Clarence Dutton eloquently described the scene: "There is a constant succession of parks and glades—dreamy avenues of grass and flowers winding between sylvan walls or spreading out into broad open meadows." These spacious bowls contain mountain muhly, blue grama, and squirrel tail grasses, and wildflowers such as lupine, yarrow, and aster.

In summer the meadows are busy places. Mountain bluebirds flash like pieces of blue sky as they snatch insects from the air. The trees ringing the meadows are riddled with woodpecker holes,

The existence of the North Rim meadows is something of a mystery. Common wisdom says they are self-sustaining grasslands, resisting encroachment by the forest. In fact, the meadows *are* filling in with trees at a fairly rapid rate. Aspen, spruce, fir, and ponderosa have moved into a dozen meadows; within a century some smaller ones will be completely consumed by trees. Several factors— exclusion of natural fires, a hundred-year warming trend, removal of livestock, and a decrease in the deer population on the Kaibab Plateau—may have favored trees over the past century.

Shrew preying on long-tailed vole.

which bluebirds recycle as their own nests. A hawk wheels overhead, training keen eyes on the slightest wrong move by a vole, which the hawk will swoop down upon and pluck up in an instant. It takes many voles to feed a hawk, which sits at the top of the food chain. The long-tailed vole (also called meadow mouse) must stay on guard for another predator, the smaller but ravenous shrew.

Small lakes are other special places on the North Rim. In the limestone caprock, collapsed sinkholes sometimes form and fill with water. These small ponds earn the name "lakes" in this mostly waterless land. They are delightful places to linger.

I did just that one autumn afternoon at Greenland Lake, watching yellow-rumped warblers fly from trees to pond and dragonflies dance over the water. A family of wild turkeys strutted up to feed. And though I didn't see them, I knew amphibians such as the Great Basin spadefoot toad and Utah tiger sala-mander might also have been present. Gopher mounds on the banks signaled the burrowings of these busy rodents.

Little Park Lake on the North Rim.

I was amazed to see a mule deer, which usually browses on shrubs, aspen, and clover, enter the water. The deer waded in cautiously at first, then deeper until up to its haunches, plunging its head underwater to sieve out aquatic plants.

In summer, it's common to see twenty, thirty, and even more deer on an evening's drive on the road along the Kaibab Plateau and the North Rim. European-American settlers gave the name Buckskin Mountain to the Kaibab Plateau, because they found Paiute Indians hunting the deer for their hides.

Mule deer eating aquatic plants.

When Teddy Roosevelt came to the North Rim in 1913 to hunt mountain lions, he labeled the cat the "destroyer of the deer . . . craven and cruel." This was a typical anthropomorphic emotion of the era—that predators were somehow evil killers and that fewer of them meant more deer. That emotion pervaded into the following decades. In the 1920s, the Kaibab deer were protected from hunting, while their major predators— wolves, coyotes, bobcats, and mountain lions—were killed as part of a wholesale,

government-sponsored predator-control program.

In July of 1913, President Theodore Roosevelt came to the Grand Canyon for a lion hunt.

As predators were systematically removed, the deer herd did explode in numbers. But the deer soon began to outstrip the food supply and then started dying off by the thousands. Today, no hunting of either the deer or their predators is allowed in the park. Although wolves never made a comeback, mountain lions have, and they are now helping keep the deer population in check.

The boreal forest community is found at cold, high elevations on the North Rim of Grand Canyon. It is a mix of conifers, including fir, spruce, and Douglas-fir, along with aspen and big grassy mountain meadows.

The ponderosa pine community, found on both rims, is in places a nearly continuous stand of tall, long-needled pines. It is a community shaped by fire and closely tied to the lives of tassel-eared squirrels.

The pinyon-juniper woodland found below the rims consists of pygmy evergreens, with a mix of chaparral shrubs. Pinyon and juniper trees depend on animals, primarily birds, for their existence.

The inner canyon is a desert of mostly low-growing, widely spaced shrubs; most dominant is blackbrush on the Tonto Platform. In years of good rainfall, wildflowers are profuse. Animals have adapted to extremes of heat and dryness.

Riparian communities in the canyon include the Colorado River, year-round streams, and springs, seeps, and waterfalls. Plants and animals of these small but significant communities cannot survive far from water.

27

Mountain lions are highly territorial. Mature solitary males and females with kittens mark the boundaries of large home ranges which they defend against transient lions, often younger males. Lions hunt alone rather than in packs, and rely on silence and surprise to catch their prey. Their hunting techniques and social structure assure there aren't too many lions or too few deer.

In nature, human values of good and evil hold no sway. What counts is survival, and deer and mountain lion have evolved with each other to accomplish that goal. Lions control deer numbers but do not cause their decline. In fact, predation strengthens deer herds by keeping them at a healthy, optimal population, by culling excess young and older, weaker animals.

As Maurice Hornocker, dean of lion research in the West, has said: "The mountain lion exerts an influence over everything below it, an influence that has evolved over millions of years."

I have yet to see a mountain lion in full glory in the wild; it is one of my fondest wishes, and the first place I would go is the Kaibab Plateau, where a fairly healthy population of lions maintains a stronghold. Estimates of numbers of lions vary widely, from perhaps 30 lions on the Kaibab to as many as 120 on the entire north side of the canyon. The presence of this supreme predator is a sign that the boreal forest is alive and well.

Ponderosa Pine Forest

On winter mornings, as I walked to work through the ponderosa pine forest on the South Rim, I was transfixed. The trunks of the stately pine trees glowed soft cinnamon, each long, green needle glimmered with a glaze of frost, and the enticing scent of vanilla lured me (no matter how foolish I might look) to put my nose in a furrow of bark and inhale the ponderosa's irresistible perfume. Lying beneath many of the trees were clumps of needles, like bushy brooms, the tips of the branches clipped off by Abert squirrels.

On warm days, the squirrels would rouse themselves from their cozy nests and scamper into the branches, delivering a sincere scolding at my intrusion. As I would soon learn, the squirrels and the pines share a very intimate relationship. The exceedingly adaptable ponderosa pines are found from British Columbia to Mexico, growing from sea level to nearly 10,000 feet elevation. On both the North and South rims of Grand Canyon, and across northern Arizona, ponderosa pines are a reliable marker of 7,000 feet elevation, where they form nearly pure stands. This drought-tolerant, sun-loving species started to become established in the Southwest at the end of the ice age, about 10,000 years ago; ponderosas rely on warm temperatures and summer rains to germinate and grow.

Abert squirrels entered the Southwest at the same time as ponderosa pine. These handsome tree squirrels are distinguished by sprightly tufts

The magnificent ponderosa pines with the rich reddish bark, called mature yellow pines, are at least 200 to 300 years old. Younger trees are often called blackjack pines for their gray-black bark. Ponderosas reach optimum seed production at about 150 years of age. Released from the big prickly cones, the ponderosa's papery, winged seeds are carried by the wind to soil where, with the right combination of conditions, they will germinate. Ideal regeneration of ponderosa requires the rare occurrence of a bumper crop of seeds in autumn, followed by a summer of generous rains. Only twice in this century have these back-to-back requirements occurred in the Southwest: in 1918-1919 and again in 1982-1983.

of fur growing from their ears, most obvious in winter. The Abert, and a cousin on the North Rim called the Kaibab squirrel, live exclusively in the ponderosa pine forest. The trees provide food and nest sites, and the squirrels perform vital service for the trees.

These tassel-eared squirrels feed on nearly every part of the ponderosa: pollen, cones, seeds, bark, and a fungus that grows on the roots.

Throughout the year, they eat the inner bark (or phloem) of ponderosa twigs. That explains those clipped branches I saw at the base of the trees. With sharp incisors, a squirrel nips off a branch, discards the needle clump, and keeps the

In presettlement times, forests of ponderosa pine consisted of large, old trees with generous grass-covered spaces between them.

twig end. The squirrel then strips away the outer bark to get to the phloem, or growing layer, of the twig, like chomping corn on the cob.

Seeds of ponderosa pine are even more of a delicacy—Abert and Kaibab squirrels partake of them from June into November. A famished squirrel can put away seventy-five seeds a day. The animal will bury some cones and return later to uncover them, using its nose to find the cache. Seeds in cones that aren't recovered may sprout into pine seedlings.

The squirrel also helps the tree with its appetite for truffles. Here, we draw in another strand of the web. Fungi called mycorrhizae (literally "fungus roots") form sheaths around a tree's roots, greatly increasing the surface area and allowing greater uptake of moisture and nutrients for the tree. Plants sustain mycorrhizae by feeding them sugar. It's what ecologists call a mutualistic relationship, apparently a critical one. Ponderosa pine, and many other plants, simply can't survive without their mycorrhizae.

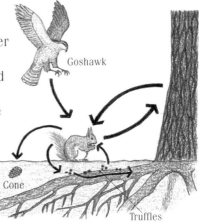

Goshawk

Cone

Truffles

After summer rains, the mycorrhizae sprout white, potato-sized fruiting bodies, the truffles squirrels find delectable. They dig up and eat the truffles, but the fungal spores pass through the squirrels' digestive tracts and are dispersed in the soil, all the better for the ponderosa pine.

This web needs one more element, a top predator. For the tassel-eared squirrels of the ponderosa forest that role is played by the northern goshawk, a hawk designed to fly in the forest. A squirrel on the ground is easy pickings for this maneuverable raptor, so the tassel-eared squirrels are safer in the trees. Abert and Kaibab squirrels build their nests fifty feet up in ponderosas, situated where the interlocking branches of several trees assure protection and escape routes. On nice winter days, a squirrel will stretch out on a tree limb like a lazy cat, remaining well hidden from a predator looking down from a higher perch.

Tree, squirrel, fungi, hawk. These are the

Mycorrhizae— fungi that grow on roots—are widespread throughout the plant world. On pines, birches, willows, and oaks, mycorrhizae form an outer sheath on the root and change its shape. In other species, the mycorrhizae actually enter root cells.

components of one of the most significant food webs within the ponderosa forest, one of perhaps a thousand webs still to be revealed.

Pinyon-Juniper Woodland & Chaparral-Scrub

A mile and a half down the Hermit Trail sits Hermit Basin, a flat area cast in an olive-green canopy of shrubby pinyon pines and Utah junipers. Called a dwarf or pygmy woodland, as if somehow unworthy, the pinyon-juniper community is to me the essence of the Southwest. True, the trees may get only twenty or thirty feet tall, but pinyons commonly live 300 or 400 years, junipers even longer. On countless occasions, these steadfast, old trees have succored me with their shade, their food, and their company.

"P-J," as it's fondly nicknamed, grows on and below the rims of the canyon from about 7,500 feet down to 4,000 feet elevation. Pinyon and juniper are supremely drought resistant, and they inhabit the lowest, driest environment of any conifers.

As I swing down the switchbacks of the Hermit Trail, I pass scrub and Gambel oaks, fendlerbush, cliffrose, sagebrush, and Mormon tea, members of the mountain scrub-chaparral community that inter- sperses with the pinyon-juniper woodland. In springtime, pink phlox tuft the limestone slopes, blue blossoms adorn tall stalks of thickleaf penstemon, and wooly-stemmed sunflowers brighten the ground.

Approaching Hermit Basin, I hear that familiar sound, the haunting calls of pinyon jays strafing the treetops. Pinyon jays and pinyon pines are entwined in an ecological marriage even tighter than that of the tassel-eared squirrels and ponderosa pines.

The short-needled pinyon of Grand Canyon is *Pinus edulis*, which means "edible pine," for the delicious, rich seeds it produces. The pinyon pine's large, brown nuts lack the wings of most pine seeds, and so cannot be dispersed by the significant agent of wind. Instead, pinyons rely completely on animals to spread their seeds and perpetuate the species. Other birds, including Clark's nutcrackers, scrub jays, and Steller's jays, along with squirrels, chipmunks, woodrats, and pinyon mice, help in this task. But pinyon jays are the real "wings" of pinyon pines.

In the dim geologic past, pinyon pines likely migrated northward from Mexico. Over millennia, bird and tree coevolved; in fact, some ecologists believe pinyon trees developed a big, wingless nut specifically to entice the birds. The jays help the tree by burying nuts in advantageous places where new pinyons can grow. And the birds derive sustenance from the seeds as well. In the spring, courting males feed pinyon nuts to the females; and after the females lay eggs, they subsist on the nuts.

Because it takes so much energy to produce such a hefty nut, pinyons don't make many nuts every year; a bumper crop is produced only every three to five years, depending on rainfall. The jays

Pinyon jays have devised ingenious techniques to harvest seeds of pinyon pines. The birds, sometimes a thousand in a flock, travel far and wide to locate cones. To get at the nuts, the jays hammer apart the green cones with their strong, tapered bills, or go for exposed seeds in open cones. A pinyon jay can tell by color, sound, and feel which seeds actually contain nuts, selecting only the dark seeds and clicking and weighing them in its bill. A jay can store up to fifty seeds in its expandable esophagus while en route to a cache site.

are excellent orchardists—they bury one to several seeds in each cache, often under tree branches and in places where snow melts early, so germination is likely. In a good year, a single flock has been known to bury four and half million

Both pinyon pines and junipers rely on animals, primarily birds, to disperse their seeds.

seeds! The birds' exceptional memories allow them to relocate the caches later and thus perpetuate this mutually beneficial relationship.

Junipers likewise rely on birds and mammals to disperse their seeds. Fleshy blue "berries," modified cones each with one or two small brown seeds, appear on the junipers in late summer. In winter, Townsend's solitaires set up shop in the woodland and defend feeding territories. Perching or hovering, a solitaire plucks juniper berries from the branches, eating as many as 240 a day. In flight, solitaires defecate and drop the seeds onto the ground where one may grow one day.

A host of other species are part of the pinyon-juniper woodland—porcupines, yuccas, bark beetles, moths, mistletoe, milkvetch, and mule deer. All can thank the pinyon jay and the Townsend's solitaire for building their home.

Desertscrub

Three thousand feet below the South Rim, a broad bench of muted gray-green slopes out to the precipitous edge of the Inner Gorge. It's called the

Tonto Platform, a hot, dry, treeless expanse partway between the rims and the river.

It's a wonderful place to walk in spring and fall, or by summer moonlight, the trail singsonging in and out of huge side canyons that anywhere else would be national parks themselves. A person can become lost in meditation on the Tonto, inspired by the widely spaced, bonsaied shrubs as perfectly arranged as an oriental garden.

Blackbrush is the most common shrub on the Tonto Platform. But, there's more variety to the

The low-growing blackbrush is hands down the dominant plant species of the Tonto Platform. When

Tonto than first meets the eye. Growing amid the blackbrush are four-wing saltbush, wolfberry, Mormon tea, turpentine broom, and prickly-pear cactus. These plants form the ecological backbone of the desert: they provide food, shelter, and nesting sites for birds, mammals, insects, and reptiles; help slow erosion of the slopes; and nurse other plant seedlings into life. Some desert shrubs are amazingly old—individuals of more than twenty species in the canyon have lived at least a hundred years.

wet, the stems are black as tar, hence the plant's name.

Still, the aridity and sparse plant life of the desert can mean lower nutrients, less organic material, and slower soil formation than in more heavily vegetated communities. By two ecological yardsticks—primary productivity (the total amount of sugar produced by plants during photosynthesis) and biomass (total weight of all the living material)—deserts rank among the lowest of the world's habitats. Because of this, food webs in the desert have often been considered simpler than in

On hot summer days in the canyon, about the only thing a person can do is sit and watch a harvester ant play the role of Sisyphus, pushing a seed, half its own size, up an incline to the colony's nest. The determination of the ant may be explained by the fact that the seed is a little package of protein and calories—and a canteen holding all the water the ant needs for the day. Ants may eat the entire seed, or they may consume only a special fat and nutrient-rich body, called an elaiosome, attached to it. They discard the seed itself, thus helping disperse the plant.

Both ants and rodents, such as pocket mice and kangaroo rats, are seed predators. Some biologists think they may be in competition for the seed supply. In lean years in the desert, such competition could become especially significant for the parties involved.

Still, ants are among the most successful organisms on the planet, some 20,000 species strong. Biologist E.O. Wilson estimates ants account for 10 percent of all the animal biomass in the Amazon rainforest, and they are only slightly less abundant in deserts, grasslands, and other parts of the world. Ants may one day inherit the earth.

other major biomes. Recent studies, however, are disproving that idea. In fact, webs can become more complex in the desert because there is much crossover between and among them. More animals are omnivores, eating not just plants or animals but both. The usual order of trophic levels can be turned topsy turvy, with predator becoming prey and vice versa. The desert's unpredictable rainfall and patchy resources also require greater adaptability.

In the exposed blackbrush community, about the only animal evident in the daytime is the black-throated sparrow. This bird lives mostly on seeds and insects and builds its nest in the forked branches of the shrubs. The other creatures you'll likely see are ants and perhaps an occasional rattlesnake. I nearly stepped on a rattler on the Tonto Trail once. Both of us were equally startled and swift in our flight. By its shyness I assumed this was *Crotalus viridis abyssus,* the Grand Canyon "pinkie," a subspecies found only in the canyon. This sweetly named rattlesnake is said to have a matching disposition, but I've never stayed around long enough to find out. *Crotalus,* the name of the genus to which rattlesnakes belong, is from the Greek word for castanet. To the Hopi Indians of northern Arizona, the sound of the rattle mimics rain falling in the desert.

Uncertainty is a fact of life for everything in this desert. All creatures must adapt to a feast-or-famine existence, competing not so much with each other but for that most precious commodity —water.

Like heat-seeking missiles, rattlesnakes have pits on their heads with which they sense the body heat of their prey—often lizards, mice, or woodrats. Rattlers mostly employ a sit-and-wait style of hunting on the ground surface. Occasionally they enter burrows, perhaps to keep cool but also to be in ideal position to nab a meal should the resident rodent return home. Rattlesnakes in turn are prey for skunks, coyotes, hawks, and even other snakes that can withstand their venom.

Western diamondback rattlesnake.

Riparian

Water. Its presence in the desert is like a soothing balm on a sore wound. Cutting through the intense desert of Grand Canyon are hundreds of streams, each as different as children in the same family. Some are seasonal, others are

Havasu Creek, one of the canyon's largest riparian areas.

perennial—their rocky streambeds are of polished pink moire and glistening gray satin. They contain still pools, veils of waterfalls, verdant hanging gardens, and grottoes and cathedrals where elves play and pray. Always they are a joy to come upon.

Wherever water flows, we find pockets of greenery that sustain unique collections of water-requiring animals. Big springs such as Thunder Spring, Roaring Spring, and Vaseys Paradise pour forth from cliffs of Redwall and Muav limestone. Mosses, monkeyflowers, maidenhair ferns, columbines, lobelia, and poison ivy cascade around them. In perennial creeks such as Bright Angel and Tapeats, soft breezes ruffle the leaves of hackberries, willows, and cottonwoods. A patch of cattails, a redbud in spring blush, a lacy catclaw

ri·par·i·an:
(rye-pear-e-an)
Of or relating to or living or located on the bank of a watercourse, as a river or stream or sometimes a lake.

38

acacia—all are signs of water. And though riparian habitat is the smallest in number of acres, it has the greatest number of species of wildlife.

Canyon treefrog with maidenhair fern.

When I think of water in the canyon I think of luxuriant hours spent watching water striders scull across eddies, while metallic damselflies dart from one horsetail rush to another. I think of the dipper, or water ouzel, bobbing on a boulder in the middle of Clear Creek, snatching up snails, caddis worms, and mayfly larvae. Though their feet are not webbed, dippers can "swim" under water in search of food. That Clear Creek dipper may have been the architect of the small nest I saw later, tucked out of harm's way behind a waterfall upstream.

I think of canyon treefrogs, like the congregation in Hermit Creek whose incessant bellowings kept me up all night. Their frantic spring mating calls resound far out of proportion to the size of these small olive-gray creatures. As amphibians, treefrogs must be near water, both to complete their breeding cycle and to keep their skin moist. They cling to slippery streamside boulders with the aid of large toe pads. Canyon treefrogs especially like flies, damselflies, and other small invertebrates. Raccoons, skunks, and ringtails patrol the streams at night, looking for a succulent treefrog or red-spotted toad.

All the streams and springs feed the mother stream, the Colorado River, the canyon's largest and most influential riparian area. The river's story is intricate, and we will hear it in the last chapter.

EDGES AND THREADS

There is no such thing as unemployment in an ecosystem.

Life is richest at the edges. Where two biotic communities come into contact, an *ecotone* exists. Travelers moving westward across the United States can see ecotones where the great deciduous forest of the East meets the Plains grassland, where grassland meets desert, and most dramatically where shoreline meets ocean. These ecological boundaries are places of transition where species can play on both sides of the fence, where diversity is greater than in either of the communities alone. It's called the edge effect.

In Grand Canyon, this effect can be seen on a smaller scale, where pinyon and juniper intermingle with ponderosa, or where spruce-fir forest meets meadow edge. Another dramatic illustration exists along the banks of the Colorado River and at the many tributaries that thread through the canyon. Here organisms often live two lives, crossing over between aquatic and terrestrial worlds to meet their needs.

Because of its unique geography, Grand Canyon shows a giant edge effect too. It is the meeting place of four major biologic provinces: the Rocky Mountain province and three of the four North American deserts. The Rocky Mountain province is represented by the conifer forests and woodlands on and just below the rims of the canyon. The deserts are the Great Basin, Mohave, and Sonoran, all found in the inner canyon.

Yet not all is intermixing at Grand Canyon. The canyon acts as a *barrier* too, for species unable to negotiate its depth, withstand the

Major deserts of North America.

ntervening desert, or cross the river. Kaibab and
Abert squirrels provide the best example. Both are
tassel-eared squirrels, close relatives with a
common ancestor. They have been isolated from
each other for at least the last 10,000 years, since
development of the ponderosa pine forest to which
they are tied. With this isolation,

MILE 40 — Great Basin
Desert

MILE 150

MILE 277

Colorado River

**Grand Canyon
National Park**

Sonoran
Desert

Mohave
Desert

A long its 277-mile
course through
Grand Canyon, the
Colorado River drops in
elevation from 3,100
feet above sea level at
Lees Ferry to 1,200 feet
at Lake Mead. Along
this elevational gradi-
ent, there is a corre-
sponding vegetational
gradient. Influences of
the Great Basin Desert
are seen down to about
river mile 40, to the
lower half of Marble

Canyon. Plants and
animals from this cold
desert include sage-
brush, shadscale, and
rabbitbrush, birds such
as sage sparrows and
sage thrashers, and the
Great Basin spadefoot
toad, Great Basin
rattlesnake, and
sagebrush lizard.

Below mile 40, mes-
quite and catclaw acacia
show up, trees of the
hot, dry Sonoran
Desert of southern
Arizona. Midway along
the rivercourse,

members of another
hot desert, the Mohave,
appear: ocotillo,
bursage, creosote bush,
Gila monsters, and
cactus wrens.

With this confluence of
major biogeographic
regions, some species
such as brittlebush
reach the limits of their
ranges.

Kaibab squirrel.

Abert squirrel.

In the last century, brittlebush has migrated upstream along the desert corridor of the inner canyon.

some genetic changes have taken place—they have developed different coloration, for example. The Kaibab squirrel is dark gray with a solid white tail, the Abert is gray with a rust stripe down its back, white belly, and white only on the underside of the tail. The Abert and Kaibab squirrels may furnish a textbook case of evolution and how species originate. If brought together, they might still be able to interbreed. But with more time apart and more genetic change, the two may one day become fully separate species. The canyon also creates a barrier for others: the Hopi rattle-snake, Arizona tiger salamander, and rock pocket mouse are confined to the south side of the canyon, while their respective counterparts, the Great Basin rattlesnake, Utah tiger salamander, and long-tailed pocket mouse, are known only on the north side.

The canyon, especially the river, serves as a *corridor* as well. By exactly replicating hundreds of photographs taken in the canyon in 1890, researcher Robert Webb has documented dramatic increases in some frost-sensitive desert plants. Uncommon a century ago along the river corridor, brittlebush is one plant now much more abundant and found up to about mile 42 on the river. Seeds may have been blown upstream, and with fewer killing frosts than formerly occurred, the shrub has been able to expand its range. Barrel cactus, prickly-pear, and a number of other cacti—all highly sensitive to freezing temperatures—have likewise shown increased densities up the river corridor.

Finally, for certain species the canyon serves as *refuge:* a sunflower known as McDougall's flaveria grows at saline springs deep in the remote western canyon. The Kanab ambersnail, an endangered species, lives among the monkeyflowers and poison ivy at only one spring in the canyon, and is known from a single other location, in southern Utah. And not to be forgotten is the Grand Canyon pink rattlesnake, found only in the inner canyon desert and nowhere else in the world. Some of these species are relicts of past climate or have highly specific environmental or reproductive requirements. In any case, all can still find a home in Grand Canyon.

Grand Canyon pink rattlesnake.

There is no such thing as unemployment in an ecosystem. Every organism has a *niche,* a job to do. If it didn't, it wouldn't be here. Each plant and animal can claim a position because it has won the adaptation game—the kangaroo rat can metabolize water from dry seeds, the rattlesnake hunts at night, the horned lizard is the color of the ground, the hummingbird's bill is designed to reach nectar deep in flowers.

Horned lizard.

Every adaptation involves physiological, behavioral, or morphologic (size, shape, color) adjustments, and each is born of the necessity to live with heat, cold, wind, drought, predators, and an endless variety of other factors. In most of

Grand Canyon, heat and dryness are overriding environmental conditions that demand adaptation. On hot days in the inner canyon, animals lay low—the jackrabbit huddles under the shade of a blackbrush, the pocket gopher burrows into the cool underground, snakes hole up in rock crevices. Most animals simply avoid the conditions, waiting until nighttime to resume their activities.

Plants, obviously, cannot move and so must bear the full brunt of the desiccating heat. To save water, blackbrush sheds leaves, going into a sort of deathwatch until conditions are more favorable. Some perennials such as sacred datura bloom only at night, when their moth pollinators are on the prowl and the day's heat has passed. Desert annuals such as phacelia, or scorpionweed, are quintessential drought evaders. They do so by compressing their life cycles. After a good rain, the annuals germinate, grow stems and leaves, bloom, set seed, then die—often in a matter of weeks. Their seeds remain dormant

It is no accident that Grand Canyon is home to more than a dozen cactus species. This family of plants is master of the art of desert adaptation. Cacti have almost done away with leaves entirely and carry on photosynthesis through their succulent stems, which are expandable, water-storing reservoirs. When rains come, the big barrel cacti in the canyon are so swollen with moisture they appear in danger of toppling over; but that moisture will sustain them through long, dry periods. A waxy cuticle covers cactus stems, minimizing loss of water to evaporation; spines, which most cacti possess, also shade and insulate the stems.

44

n the soil, sometimes for years, awaiting the next favorable period of rainfall and temperature.

Plants and animals must also adapt to cold, especially in the rim forests. As winter approaches, many birds, including raptors and songbirds, simply pack up and leave. Hawks, hummingbirds, and others undertake long-distance fall migrations to warmer, southern climes. Townsend's solitaires and Clark's nutcrackers don't go so far; taking advantage of the canyon's elevational differences, they move from the forest down into the pinyon-juniper woodland and the inner canyon. Mammals do the same; mule deer migrate on well-defined routes into the P-J where they browse heavily on cliffrose. In autumn, thousands of monarch butterflies flutter away to wintering grounds in Mexico. Snakes and lizards slow their metabolism, entering a state called torpor.

Among plants, the primary adaptation to cold is the conifer's evergreen habit, which allows them to photosynthesize whenever air temperatures are right. The resin in their needles acts like antifreeze, and the spire shape and flexible branches let them shed snow.

The adaptation game never ends. Throughout Earth's long history, a cast of winners and losers, has-beens and might-have-beens, has come and gone. Evolution is a continuous round of experiments, in Grand Canyon we have the privilege of seeing an extraordinary natural diversity that has resulted.

Cactus look-alikes
A group of plants in Africa called euphorbias look very much like cacti, with spiny armor and succulent habit. This is an example of convergent evolution, in which unrelated species have found the same solutions to similar environmental problems.

Cold temperatures and heavy snowfall at the higher elevations of the canyon in winter require adaptability on the part of plants and animals.

TORN WEBS

It's tricky trying to play Mother Nature, and the long-term ecological effect ...must be monitored.

In the milky waters at the mouth of the Little Colorado River, the silver body of a small fish flashes in the current. It's late spring, the time when this fish must perform her duty to her species and find a suitable place to lay eggs and produce young.

In the old days, this fish with a pointed head and strange-looking humped back could find many good spawning sites on the Colorado River. But not now. About the only warm, safe place left in Grand Canyon is where the Little Colorado joins the main Colorado.

The reason for the fish's plight is that the Colorado River has changed. In 1963, the gates of Glen Canyon Dam on the border of Arizona and Utah were closed. Downstream in Grand Canyon the Colorado River was altered dramatically and irrevocably. In the heyday of our fish, called a humpback chub, the river flowed rusty brown with sediments, "too thick to drink and too thin to plow," they used to say. In the old *Río Colorado,* water temperatures and flows varied with the seasons.

Since the gates of Glen Canyon Dam were closed in 1963, the ecology of the Colorado River downstream in Grand Canyon has changed dramatically and irrevocably.

Now, nearly all the Colorado's sediment settles to the bottom of Lake Powell, formed by the ten-million-ton concrete dam. Water is released through the dam's penstocks from 200 feet below the lake's surface. Now the Colorado downstream from the dam flows clear and green as an emerald,

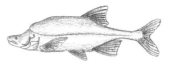

and stays at a constant, chilly forty-eight degrees Fahrenheit. The water level in the Colorado in Grand Canyon now fluctuates daily rather than seasonally, almost entirely in response to demand for electrical power generated at the dam and distributed to cities throughout the Southwest.

With these fundamental hydrologic alterations came equally fundamental, and swift, changes in the Colorado River's ecosystem. At every level of the aquatic food chain, plants and animals were affected. Native fish such as the humpback chub, for the past two million years perfectly attuned to the murky turbulence of desert rivers, have now found refuge only at the mouth of the Little Colorado and in warmer backwaters of the Colorado. Other native fish did not fare as well—roundtail and bonytail chubs and the Colorado squawfish are now extinct in Grand Canyon, and the razorback sucker is so rare it is for all practical purposes considered extirpated.

Four species of native fish still live in the post-dam Colorado River in Grand Canyon. Their numbers are viable but precarious. From top: humpback chub, flannelmouth sucker, bluehead sucker, and speckled dace.

Such changes can be traced back to the source of the food web, sunlight, which now penetrates the clear water and nourishes a healthy crop of algae. *Cladophora,* the most abundant algae, attach to rocks on the stream bed, and in the long, silky tresses live millions of microscopic algae called diatoms. The diatoms nourish worms, midges, flies, and especially a crustacean called *Gammarus* that looks like a small crayfish.

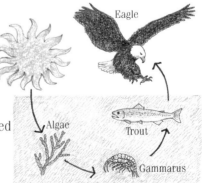

Gammarus—introduced to feed another nonnative animal, rainbow trout—now dominates the invertebrate community in the river's altered food chain. Although stocking of nonnative trout has ceased in the park, the trout continue to reproduce and find the cold, clear waters of the new Colorado much to their liking. As it happens, the trout and other nonnative fish also prey on and compete with native humpback chubs.

In recent years, rainbow trout have attracted a "glamour" predator to Grand Canyon—the bald eagle. Though migrating eagles were known to pass through the canyon, they usually did not tarry, until they discovered a feast in the form of spawning trout at the mouth of Nankoweap Creek, a tributary entering the Colorado in Marble Canyon.

In winters in the late 1980s and early 1990s, shivering researchers roosted high in the cliffs all day observing the behavior of spawning trout and hungry bald eagles. At the peak of the spawn in late February to mid March, some 1,500 trout congregated at the mouth of the stream, and more than twenty eagles a day successfully hunted them. The only competition the eagles encountered was from pirate ravens. One wily raven would distract the eagle with a rear attack, while the other in front snatched the trout right out of the eagle's mouth.

As well as being a sediment sink, Lake Powell has also become a phosphorous sink. This critical nutrient gets downstream only in limited amounts, and is quickly taken up by algae in the Colorado just below Glen Canyon Dam. Almost no phosphorous is left to nourish plant growth farther downstream. At the western end of Grand Canyon, in Lake Mead, researchers documented sharp declines in plant productivity, eventually hurting striped bass and shad, fish once abundant there. To fix this, fertilizer has been added artificially to Lake Mead to replace that lost to Lake Powell.

Phosphorous, along with carbon and nitrogen, is a critical nutrient cycling through an ecosystem. It comes not from the atmosphere but from the weathering of rocks.

The ripple effects so often felt throughout a food web may be responsible for the recovery of a once-endangered top predator of the river. Floating down a long, quiet stretch of river one day in Marble Canyon, I heard a high-pitched, almost mechanical sound echoing off the canyon walls. As we came closer, I realized the unearthly sound was made by a peregrine falcon up in a cliff aerie.

In the 1960s, peregrine populations everywhere had dropped precipitously due to reproductive losses caused by the pesticide DDT. Peregrines were listed as endangered, DDT use was banned in the United States, and recovery efforts were undertaken. The falcons have made a stunning comeback, and Grand Canyon is a center of that startling recovery. More peregrines have been counted in the canyon than anywhere else in the lower forty-eight states, and their nests have been found every few miles along the river.

Though the DDT ban can undoubtedly explain

Peregrine falcon.

much of this revival, biologists think that, as with bald eagles, the changes brought about by Glen Canyon Dam may have benefited peregrine falcons in the canyon. With increased numbers of midges, flies, and gnats, there is more food for insect-eating wildlife, including bats, swifts, swallows, and waterfowl, all favorite prey of peregrines.

Tamarisk is a successful newcomer to riparian areas in the inner canyon.

The effects of Glen Canyon Dam have also extended to the riparian area bordering the river. A new zone of plant life has grown up along the shore. Most notable among the newcomers is an Old World tree called tamarisk, a real survivor and tough competitor with native plants such as coyote willow.

Many people have a distinct disdain for tamarisk because it is nonnative, is such a prolific reproducer, and forms impenetrable thickets. But tamarisk has provided habitat for a bevy of insects, including dragonflies, cicadas, and leafhoppers given to periodic large outbreaks. All sorts of riparian birds and other animals have taken advantage of this abundant food, including Bell's vireos and endangered southwestern willow flycatchers.

While the pros and cons of Glen Canyon Dam are weighed and its operations altered to protect downstream resources, what has emerged is the realization that a naturalized, as opposed to a natural, ecosystem has evolved in and along the Colorado River in Grand Canyon. It is likely too late to turn back the clock for the Colorado River, at least in any foreseeable human lifetimes. This situation raises difficult questions for those whose mandate is to manage the indigenous resources of a national park in a "natural" state. Biologist Bryan Brown succinctly posed the dilemma: "How should management respond when an endangered native bird [southwestern willow flycatcher] is nesting in exotic vegetation [tamarisk] in a man-made environment and is threatened with human-caused changes to its habitat?" Obviously there are no easy answers.

While the addition of a dam has forever altered the ecological landscape of the Colorado River, the subtraction of another kind of disturbance has had equally profound effects elsewhere in Grand Canyon. The disturbance is fire, a natural force in the evolution of all the canyon's plant communities, especially the forests.

Complete suppression of fire was once a conscious policy of land-managing agencies, mainly because fire was viewed as a bad, destructive thing. Now, ecologists and resource managers are seeing fire as friend rather than foe. The reason for the switch is the growing recognition that fire benefits forests.

Fire scars on cross sections of trees clearly show when the period of suppression began about a

For eight days in the spring of 1996, a flow of 45,000 cubic feet per second was released from Glen Canyon Dam. The high flow was an experiment to stir up sediment on the riverbed and deposit it

on shore, distribute nutrients, restore backwaters for native fish and other animals, and re-create dynamics of the Colorado River ecosystem before the dam was built. Scientists will continue studies to assess whether those multiple aims were achieved.

This cross section of a ponderosa tree shows an average of 25 fires in a 100-year cycle.

hundred years ago, and how often fires burned through the forest naturally before that time. In the park's ponderosa forest in pre-settlement times, fires burned with remarkable frequency—every seven to ten years on average. Lightning was the big match that started these fires; if lightning struck a tall tree in spring, the fires might burn for several months during the dry, early summer. About 8,000 acres burned in an average year.

In the spruce-fir forest, fires burned less frequently, about every 70 to 250 years. Spruce and fir have not adapted to fire to the extent ponderosa have; their bark is thin, and they possess flammable pockets of resin. Consequently, they are more vulnerable to fire.

Ponderosa pines, on the other hand, are highly adapted and resistant to fire. Older trees have thick, insulative bark; seeds germinate on the mineral soils created by fire; saplings can withstand hot fires; and the trees self-prune lower branches so fire doesn't have a ladder along which to climb into the crowns. Ponderosa stands were thinned by the frequent fires, which created the open, parklike feeling of the forest that caught the eyes of many early visitors to the canyon. Fire makes openings, restores a mosaic of young and old plants, and returns nutrients to the soil. It keeps the forest in good health.

In the absence of fire, the forest has become crowded with "doghair" thickets of younger trees, almost all the same age, that germinated in wet years. The heavy buildup of needles and duff at the base of mature trees makes them vulnerable to fire by killing their surface roots. Downed trees and woody branches have added fuel, essentially leaving the forest a tinderbox waiting to explode. Rather than cooler, lighter ground fires, as occurred in the past, fires now are likely to burn hotter and faster, reaching the crowns of trees and causing far more long-lasting damage.

The big question is how to judiciously reintroduce this major influence in forests that have not burned for a century. On nearly 90 percent of the park's acreage, naturally ignited fires are allowed to burn if they fall within certain "prescriptions" of temperature, humidity, wind, and other conditions. To reduce especially high fuel loads, park managers are actually setting fires in some places, again within the bounds of specific prescriptions. It's tricky trying to play Mother Nature, and the long-term ecological effects of fire must be monitored before we'll know what is really happening.

In selected parts of Grand Canyon, park managers set "prescribed" fires to reduce the fuel load of the forest and restore fire's natural role in the ecosystem.

EPILOG

And so we begin to see some of the complexities of the ecosystem called Grand Canyon.

And so we begin to see some of the complexities of the ecosystem called Grand Canyon—a few of the components, their fined-tuned relationships, and how those relationships can be altered, either knowingly or unknowingly. Although the canyon has undeniably been affected by human action, it still functions as a healthy, intact, living system.

One winter I hiked down the South Kaibab Trail, took a right on the Tonto Trail, and walked into the first big arm of Cremation Creek. In sheltered overhangs of Tapeats Sandstone, I had a kitchen, a bedroom, and a sitting room. There I spent a snug night, out of the elements, in complete contentment. It was a cold day when I hiked back out. As I labored up the steep trail, a coyote howled out of the gray mists, back where I'd come from. I listened to the chorus, smiling, reveling in the feeling of having the entire Grand Canyon to myself. Just me and that coyote, knowing our spirits belong to this canyon home.

The ethical imperative should therefore be, first of all, prudence. We should judge every scrap of biodiversity as priceless while we learn to use it and come to understand what it means to humanity.

—E.O. Wilson, naturalist

Readings

Brown, Bryan, Steven W. Carothers, R. Roy Johnson. *Grand Canyon Birds.* University of Arizona Press, Tucson. 1987.

Carothers, Steven W. and Bryan T. Brown. *The Colorado River Through Grand Canyon.* University of Arizona Press, Tucson. 1991.

Euler, Robert C. ed. *The Archaeology, Geology, and Paleobiology of Stanton's Cave.* Monograph Number 6, Grand Canyon Natural History Association, Grand Canyon. 1984.

Hoffmeister, Donald F. *Mammals of Grand Canyon.* University of Illinois Press, Urbana. 1971.

Lanner, Ronald M. *The Piñon Pine: A Natural and Cultural History.* University of Nevada Press, Reno. 1981.

Miller, Donald M. et al. *Amphibians and Reptiles of the Grand Canyon.* Monograph Number 4. Grand Canyon Natural History Association, Grand Canyon. 1982.

Moore, Margaret. "Tree Encroachment on Meadows of the North Rim of Grand Canyon National Park." Final Report, National Park Service #CA 8000-8-0002. May 1994.

Murphy, Alexandra. *Graced by Pines: The Ponderosa Pine in the American West.* Mountain Press, Missoula, Montana. 1994.

Polis, Gary A. ed. *The Ecology of Desert Communities.* University of Arizona Press, Tucson. 1991.

Schmidt, Jeremy. *Grand Canyon National Park: A Natural History Guide.* Houghton Mifflin, Boston. 1993.

Stevens, Larry. *The Colorado River in Grand Canyon: A Guide.* Red Lake Books, Flagstaff, Arizona. 1983.

Warren, Peter L. et al. "Vegetation of Grand Canyon National Park." Technical Report No. 9, Cooperative National Park Resources Studies Unit, University of Arizona, Tucson. 1982.

Webb, Robert. *Grand Canyon, A Century of Environmental Change.* University of Arizona Press, Tucson. 1996.

Wilson, E.O. *The Diversity of Life.* W.W. Norton, New York. 1992.

Zwinger, Ann Haymond. *Downcanyon: A Naturalist Explores the Colorado River through the Grand Canyon.* University of Arizona Press, Tucson. 1995.

About the Author

Rose Houk lived at Grand Canyon National Park for two years, working as a ranger naturalist and publications assistant. Now based in Flagstaff, Arizona, she writes books and articles that often focus on natural history and national parks. Other publications on Grand Canyon include a *Guide to the South Kaibab Trail* and a chapter on the Colorado River for Reader's Digest Books.

Photography Credits

Tom Bean: p. 11, 28, 43 (top); Shirley A. Briggs: p. 9, courtesy the Rachel Carson History Project; Robert M. Butterfield: p. 17; Michael Collier: p. 25, 38, 42, 50; George H.H. Huey: cover and p. 4, 5, 7, 12 (both), 15, 22, 23, 24, 30, 34, 35, 37, 39, 43 (bottom), 45, 49, 51, 54; Kaibab National Forest: p. 52; Museum of Northern Arizona Photo Archives (neg. H17.18/67.107): p. 18; National Park Service: p. 25, 53.